Contents

The English dice ----------------------- 2

The body --------------------------- 3

Clothes ----------------------------- 4

Drinks ------------------------------ 6

The farm --------------------------- 8

Fruit -------------------------------- 10

Pet animals ------------------------- 12

The restaurant ---------------------- 14

The sea ----------------------------- 16

Sport -------------------------------- 18

The supermarket -------------------- 20

The town --------------------------- 22

Transport --------------------------- 24

Vegetables -------------------------- 26

The weather ------------------------- 27

The zoo ----------------------------- 28

The English dice

To make the dice:

Photocopy or trace the dice.

With an adult cut out the dice.

Fold down the sections marked x.

Fold the lines in between the dice faces.

Fold the dice together, and glue the sections marked x.

three

six

five **four** **two**

one

To play the English number game:

Role the dice, and say in English the number you get.

The next player roles the dice, and says the number they get.

Whoever gets the biggest number in each round gets a point, and if two players get the same number they both get a point.

The winner is the first person to get five points.

The body

The idea of this game is to be the first to draw a robot. Roll the dice, and say the English word for the part of the robot's body for the number of the dice you have thrown. Draw the part of the robot and write the English word if you haven't got this word yet. Take turns to roll the dice. To draw a complete robot you will need to throw 3, 4, 5 and 6 twice.

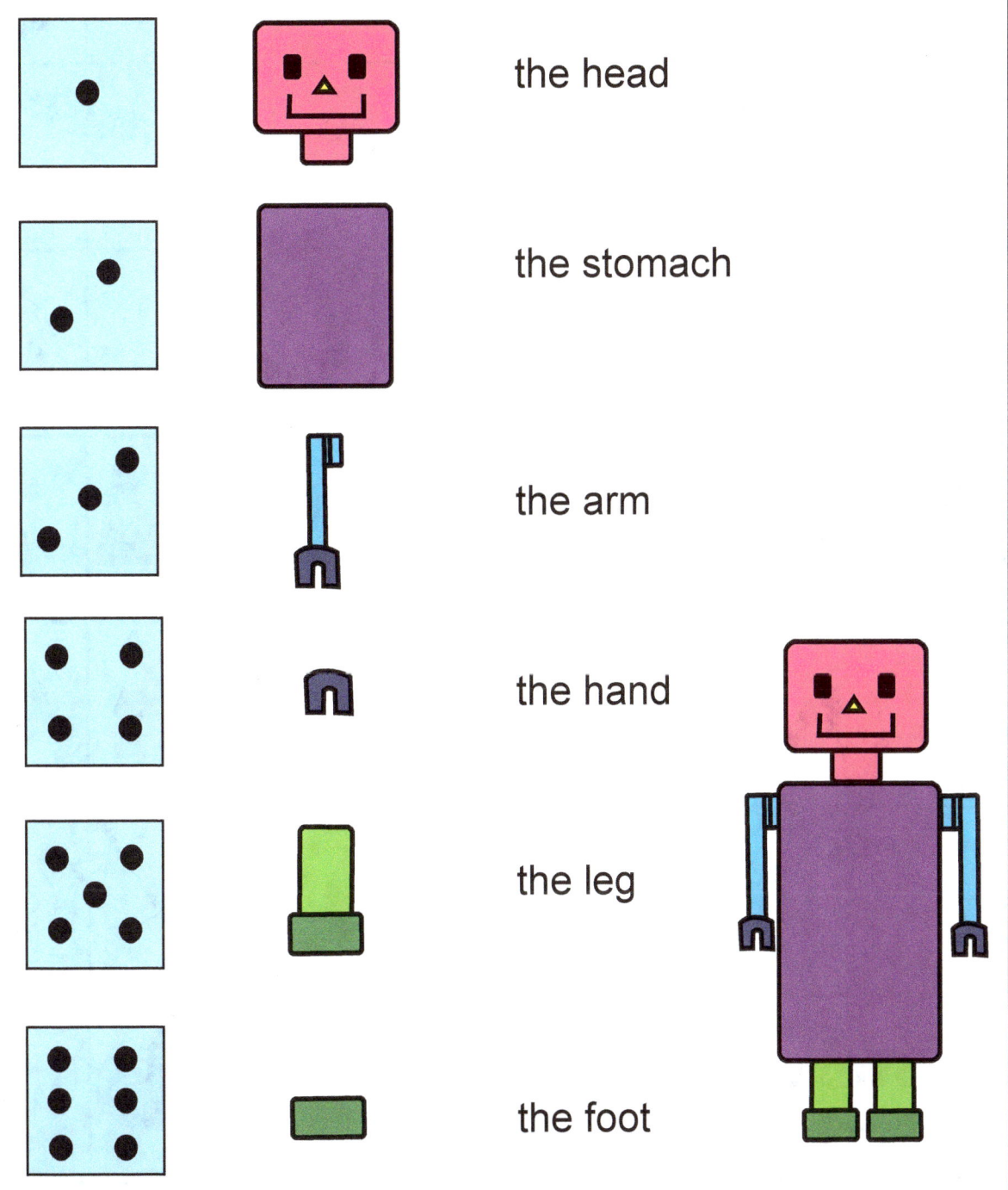

the head

the stomach

the arm

the hand

the leg

the foot

Clothes

For the snakes & ladders game you will need:

A **dice** (You can use a normal dice or make the dice on page 2.)

A **counter** for **each player** (You can use cubes, rubbers or make your own.)

To play:

Place all the counters on **Start**.

The first player rolls the dice, and counts that number of spaces.

If there is a ladder in the final square, go up it.

If there is a snake in the final square, go down it.

Say in English what is in the final square you land on.

Take turns to roll the dice. To win, be the first to reach **Finish**.

  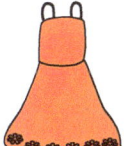

a jumper   a t-shirt   a dress

  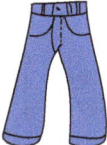

a skirt   trousers   jeans

Drinks

For this 2 page game you will need: A dice and a counter for each player. (You can use cubes, rubbers or make your own counters.)

a coke   a lemonade   a water

To play: Place all the counters on **Start**. The first player rolls the dice, and counts that number of spaces. Say in English what is in the final square you land on. Take turns to roll the dice. To win, be the first to reach **Finish**.

a coffee   a tea   an orange juice   an apple juice

The farm

For this game you will need:

A **dice** (You can use a normal dice or make the dice on page 2.)
A **counter for each player** (You can use cubes, rubbers or make your own.)
A piece of paper and a pencil for each player.

Imagine you are going to a farm, and want to visit the animals at the farm. To win, you need to be the first to visit the following six animals:

a bull   a cow   a pig

a chicken   a chick   a sheep

To play:

Place your counter on **Start**. Roll the dice and move your counter that number of spaces. Count the number of spaces in English.

1	2	3	4	5	6
one	two	three	four	five	six

If you arrive at one of the animals, say the English word for the animal, and write the word in English if you haven't written it yet. Take turns to roll the dice.

If you arrive at a moon you have to miss a go.

Who will be the first to visit all six animals?

Fruit

For the fruit game you will need:
A **dice** (You can use a normal dice or make the dice on page 2.)
A **counter for each player** (You can use cubes, rubbers or make your own.)

To play:

Place all the counters on **Start**.

The first player rolls the dice, and counts that number of spaces.

Say in English what is in the final square you land on.

Take turns to roll the dice. To win, be the first to reach **Finish**.

an apple   an orange   a banana

      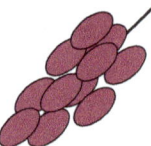

a pear   a melon   grapes

Pet animals

For the snakes & ladders game you will need:
A **dice** (You can use a normal dice or make the dice on page 2.)
A **counter for each player** (You can use cubes, rubbers or make your own.)

To play:

Place all the counters on **Start**.

The first player rolls the dice, and counts that number of spaces.

If there is a ladder in the final square, go up it.

If there is a snake in the final square, go down it.

Say in English what is in the final square you land on.

Take turns to roll the dice. To win, be the first to reach **Finish**.

a cat   a tortoise   a dog

a horse   a rabbit   a hamster

The restaurant

For this game you will need:

A **dice** (You can use a normal dice or make the dice on page 2.)

A **counter for each player** (You can use cubes, rubbers or make your own.)

To play:

Place all the counters on **Start**. The first player rolls the dice, and counts that number of spaces. Say in English what is in the final space you land on. Take turns to roll the dice. To win, be the first to reach **Finish**.

The sea

For the sea game you will need:
A **dice** (You can use a normal dice or make the dice on page 2.)
A **counter for each player** (You can use cubes, rubbers or make your own.)

To play:

Place all the counters on **Start**.

The first player rolls the dice, and counts that number of spaces.

Say in English what is in the final square you land on.

Take turns to roll the dice. To win, be the first to reach **Finish**.

 a dolphin

 a shark   If you land on **a shark** go back to the beginning!

 an octopus   If you land on **an octopus** miss a go!

 a seagull

 a penguin

 a fish

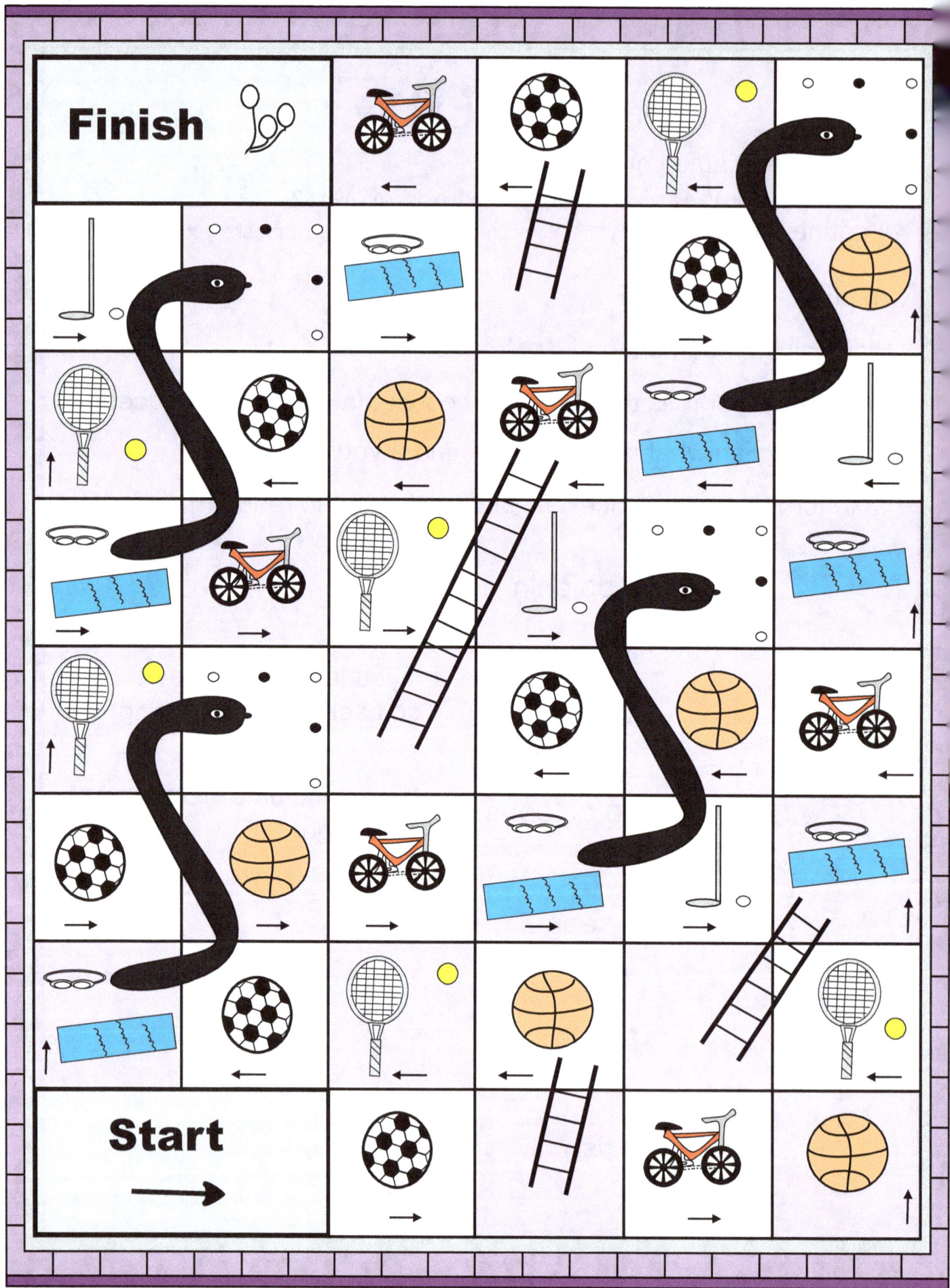

Sport

For the snakes & ladders game you will need:
A dice (You can use a normal dice or make the dice on page 2.)
A counter for each player (You can use cubes, rubbers or make your own.)

To play:

Place all the counters on **Start**.

The first player rolls the dice, and counts that number of spaces.

If there is a ladder in the final square, go up it.

If there is a snake in the final square, go down it.

Say in English what is in the final square you land on.

Take turns to roll the dice. To win, be the first to reach **Finish**.

football   tennis   basketball

swimming   cycling   mini-golf

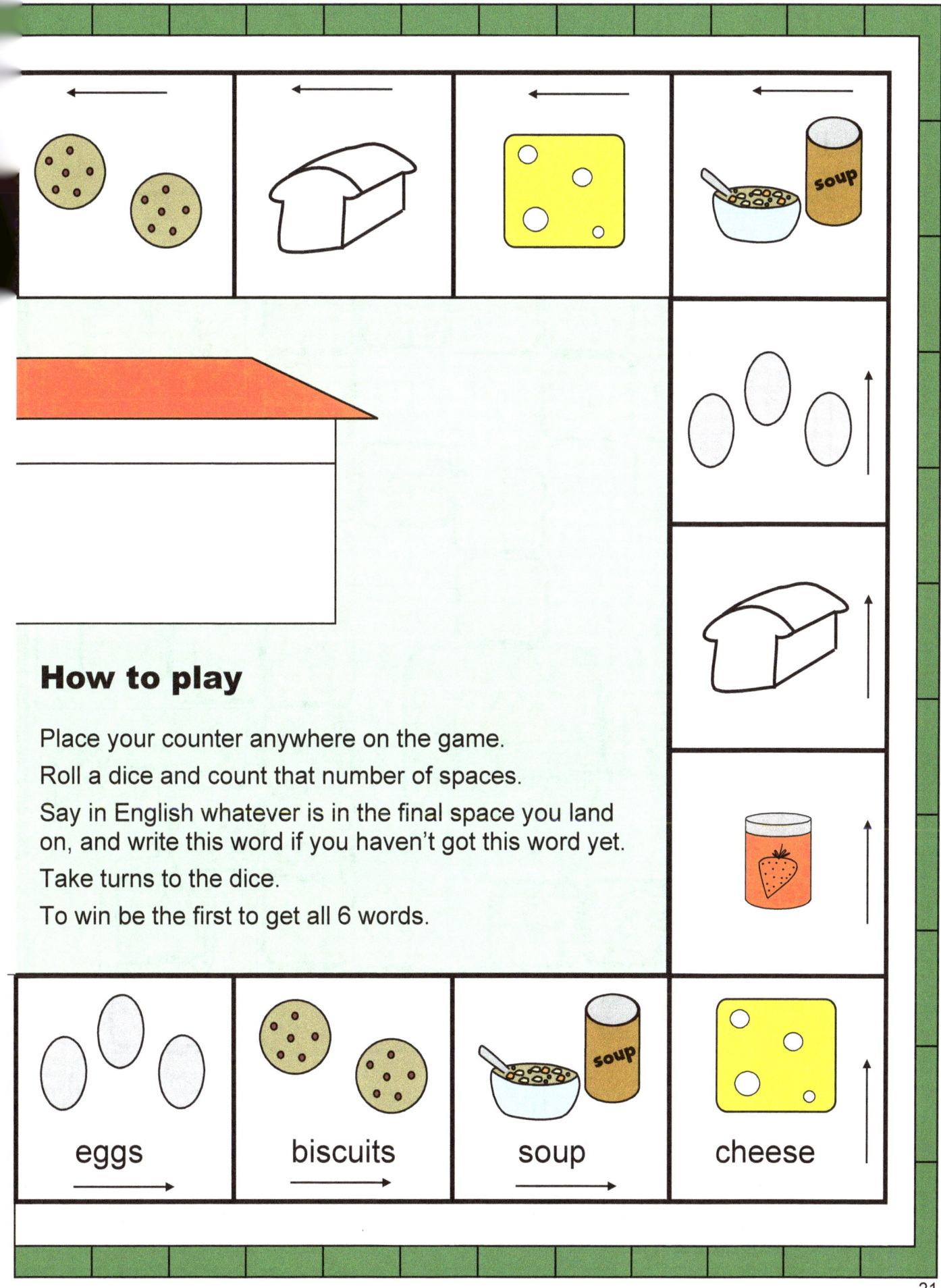

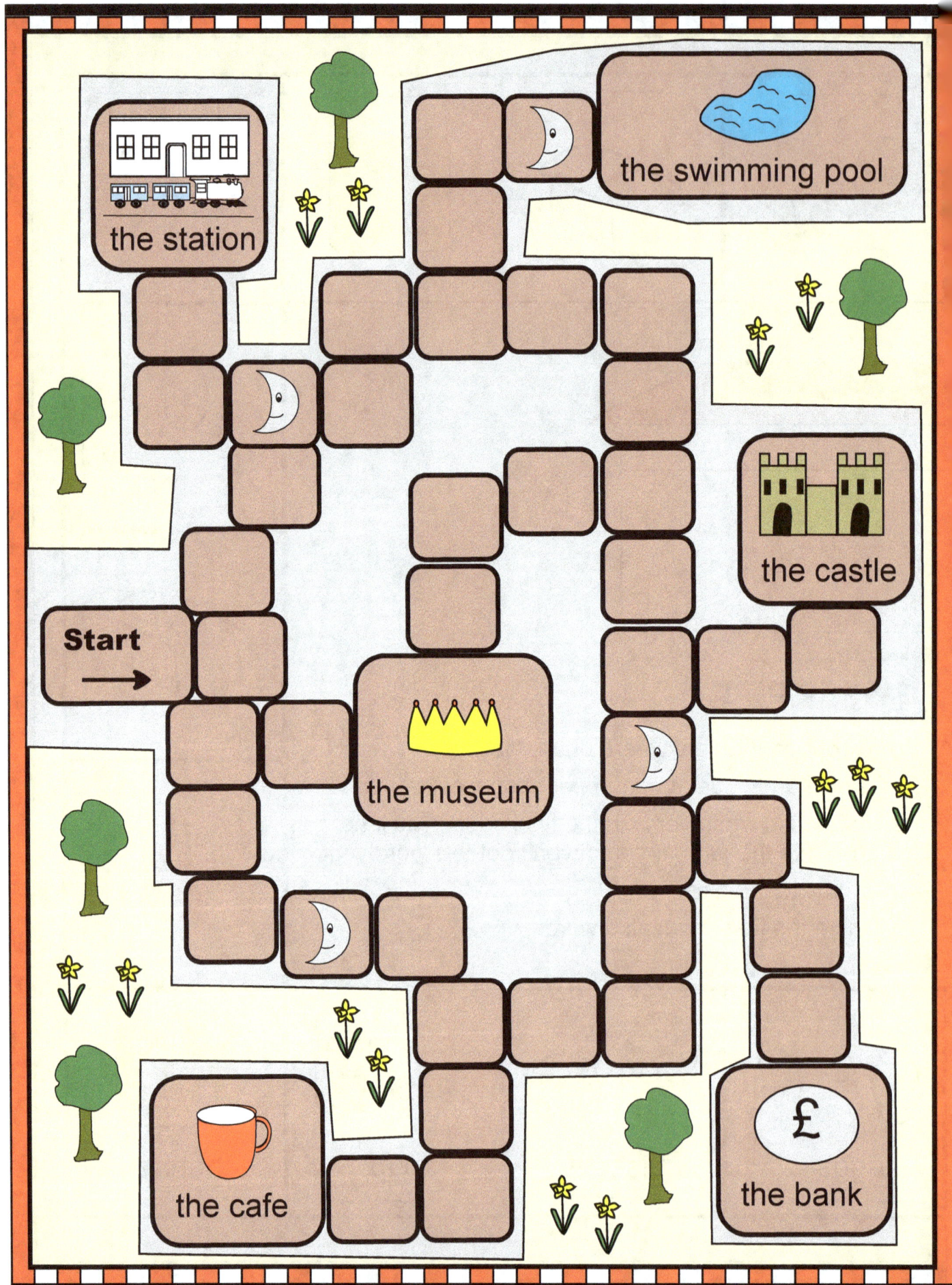

The town

Imagine you are on holiday, and want to go to some places in the town where you are staying. To win, you need to be the first person to go to the following six places:

the swimming pool   the station   the bank

the castle   the museum   the cafe

To play:

Place your counter on **Start**. Roll the dice and move your counter that number of spaces. Count the number of spaces in English.

1	2	3	4	5	6
one	two	three	four	five	six

If you arrive at one of the places, say the English word for the place, and if you haven't been there yet, draw the place and write the word in English.

If you arrive at a moon you have to miss a go.

Take turns to roll the dice. Who will be the first to visit all six places?

Transport

For the transport board game you will need:
A **dice** (You can use a normal dice or make the dice on page 2.)
A **counter for each player** (You can use cubes, rubbers or make your own.)

To play:

Place all the counters on **Start**.

Roll the dice, and count that number of spaces.

Say in English what is in the final square you land on.

Take turns to roll the dice. To win, be the first to reach **Finish.**

a car   a plane   a bus

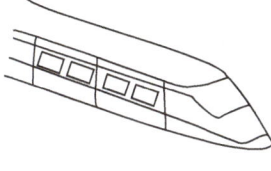  

a train   a boat   a bike

Vegetables

Guess the English word

Each player chooses one of the English words from above. You can secretly write down your word if you want to. Take turns to guess the words of the other player or players. If you guess the word correctly, you win a point. Then everyone chooses a new word. To win, be the first person to get 5 points.

Alternative game: Take turns to draw one of the above. The other players have to guess the English word.

The weather

For the weather pairs game you will need to photocopy this page 2 or 4 times. Then, with an adult cut out the 8 cards per page. (Or make your own cards by copying the pictures and words.)

To play: Place the cards face down. Take turns to choose two cards, saying the English weather phrase. Keep the cards that match and turn over the cards that don't. Who will win the most cards?

The zoo

Number of players: 2   Each player will need 5 counters
(The counters can be cubes, rubbers, or home made on pieces of paper.)

Take turns to place one of your counters on the board as you say in English the zoo animal you choose.

To win you need to get three counters in a row either vertically, horizontally or diagonally.

© Joanne Leyland 2022

The pages in this book may be photocopied for use at home or at school by the purchaser or purchasing institution only. They may not be reproduced electronically.